SPORTS
CHAMPIONSHIPS

BY ALLAN MOREY

THE WORLD CUP

TORQUE™

BELLWETHER MEDIA · MINNEAPOLIS, MN

Are you ready to take it to the extreme? Torque books thrust you into the action-packed world of sports, vehicles, mystery, and adventure. These books may include dirt, smoke, fire, and chilling tales. **WARNING** : read at your own risk.

This edition first published in 2019 by Bellwether Media, Inc.

No part of this publication may be reproduced in whole or in part without written permission of the publisher. For information regarding permission, write to Bellwether Media, Inc., Attention: Permissions Department, 6012 Blue Circle Drive, Minnetonka, MN 55343.

Library of Congress Cataloging-in-Publication Data

Names: Morey, Allan, author.
Title: The World Cup / by Allan Morey.
Description: Minneapolis, Minnesota : Bellwether Media, Inc., 2019. | Series:
   Torque: Sports Championships | Includes bibliographical references and
   index. | Audience: Ages: 7-12. | Audience: Grades: 3 through 7.
Identifiers: LCCN 2018001811 (print) | LCCN 2018003384 (ebook) |
   ISBN 9781626178670 (hardcover : alk. paper) | ISBN 9781618914873
   (paperback : alk. paper) | ISBN 9781681036083 (ebook)
Subjects: LCSH: World Cup (Soccer)–History–Juvenile literature. |
   Soccer–History–Juvenile literature.
Classification: LCC GV943.49 (ebook) | LCC GV943.49 .M676 2019 (print) |
   DDC 796.334/668–dc23
LC record available at https://lccn.loc.gov/2018001811

Editor: Rebecca Sabelko   Designer: Jon Eppard

Printed in the United States of America, North Mankato, MN.

TABLE OF CONTENTS

Hat Trick!...................................4

What Is the World Cup?........6

History of the World Cup...10

Road to the World Cup........14

Superfans...............................20

Glossary.................................22

To Learn More......................23

Index......................................24

HAT TRICK!

It is the summer of 2015. The United States Women's National Team faces Japan in the World Cup final **match**.

CARLI LLOYD ·····>

4

The U.S. starts off strong. Carli Lloyd knocks in a corner kick from Megan Rapinoe. Lloyd scores again minutes later. Then, she scores an incredible goal from midfield! It is a **hat trick**! The U.S. wins 5–2. They are World Cup champs!

WHAT IS THE WORLD CUP?

The World Cup is a championship soccer **tournament**. The International Federation of Football Association (FIFA) organizes this tournament.

More than 200 teams are members of FIFA. Teams from member countries compete to **qualify** for the World Cup tournament. The winner of the World Cup receives the FIFA World Cup Trophy.

ALL ABOUT THE RULES

FIFA was founded in 1904. The organization established a common set of rules so teams around the world could play each other.

WOMEN'S FIFA ·····▶
WORLD CUP
TROPHY

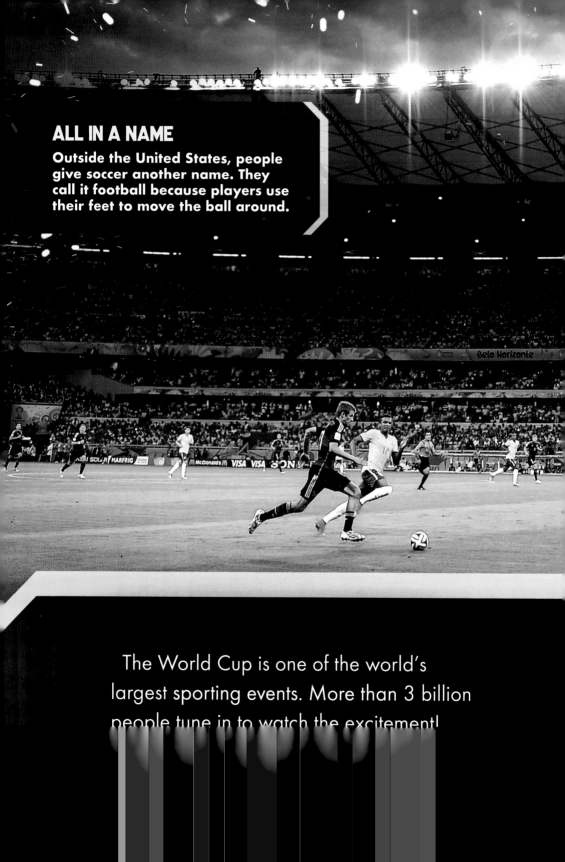

ALL IN A NAME

Outside the United States, people give soccer another name. They call it football because players use their feet to move the ball around.

The World Cup is one of the world's largest sporting events. More than 3 billion people tune in to watch the excitement!

There is a men's and women's World Cup.
These tournaments take place every four
years. The women's tournament is played the
year after the men's. Different countries host

HISTORY OF THE WORLD CUP

In the early 1900s, soccer became an Olympic sport. This helped it become more popular. It also led FIFA to plan a world championship tournament.

TEAM SPORT

Soccer was one of the first team sports to be part of the Olympics.

1924 OLYMPIC MATCH

1930 WORLD CUP TOURNAMENT

The first men's World Cup tournament was held in 1930. There were only 13 teams. Uruguay's national team beat Argentina 4–2 in the final match. The U.S. finished third.

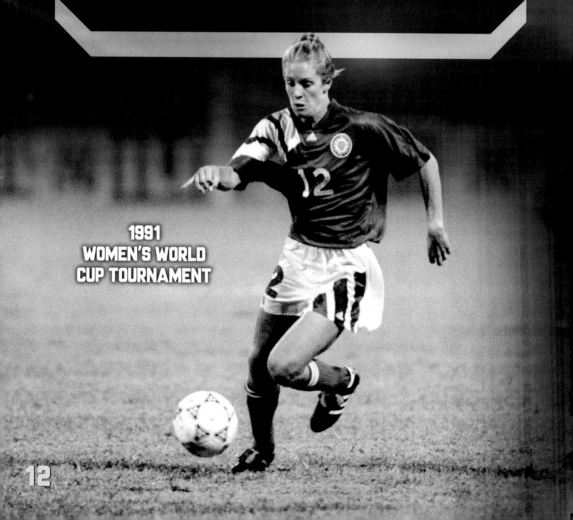

The World Cup's popularity has continued to grow since 1930. In 1982, 24 teams played in the tournament. FIFA has since increased the number of teams to 32.

In 1991, FIFA organized the first women's World Cup tournament. The U.S. National Team beat Norway 2–1 in the final match.

1991 WOMEN'S WORLD CUP TOURNAMENT

WORLD CUP CHAMPS

(MEN)
BRAZIL

1958, 1962, 1970, 1994, 2002

WORLD CUP MVP ·········▶

Pelé is the only men's player to win three World Cups.

PELÉ

(WOMEN)
UNITED STATES

1991, 1999, 2015

WORLD CUP MVP ·········▶

Mia Hamm helped the U.S. National Team win two World Cups. She was also FIFA's World Player of the Year in 2001 and 2002.

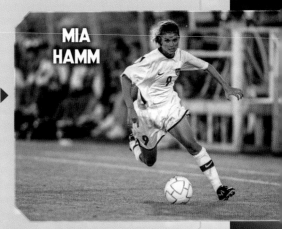

MIA HAMM

ROAD TO THE WORLD CUP

The qualification round for the World Cup starts years before the final match. National teams from around the world are divided into six **regions**. Teams in each region play one another in qualifying matches.

Only the best teams in each region make it to the World Cup tournament. There are just 32 spots in the final round.

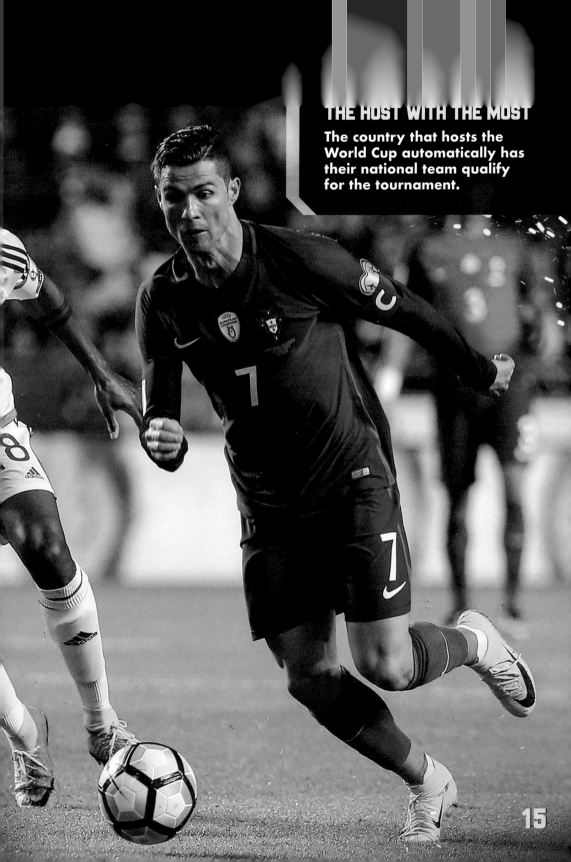

THE HOST WITH THE MOST

The country that hosts the World Cup automatically has their national team qualify for the tournament.

The final round has two stages. In the group stage, teams are divided into eight groups of four. The teams in each group play each other. The 2 best teams in each group move on to the **knockout stage**.

These remaining 16 teams are placed into a **bracket**. Only the winning teams from each round move on. They play until 2 teams face each other in the final match.

WORLD CUP TOURNAMENT BRACKET

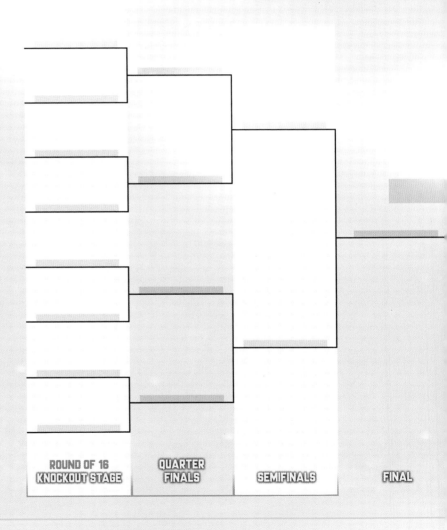

ROUND OF 16
KNOCKOUT STAGE

QUARTER
FINALS

SEMIFINALS

FINAL

WORLD CUP CHAMPION

FINAL

SEMIFINALS

QUARTER
FINALS

ROUND OF 16
KNOCKOUT STAGE

SUPERFANS

Soccer fans are some of the wildest in the world! They dress up in their country's colors. They paint their faces and color their hair. Fans wave national flags to support their teams.

VUVUZELA

The vuvuzela is a long horn instrument. Fans would blow them so loudly at matches that they were banned from the 2014 World Cup.

Soccer fans are also some of the loudest. They sing special chants to cheer on their teams. The wild fans are just one reason to watch the World Cup!

GLOSSARY

bracket—the pairing up of opponents in a tournament

hat trick—when one player scores three goals

knockout stage—a stage in a tournament during which only the winning teams move on

match—a soccer game

qualify—to earn a spot in a tournament

regions—areas

tournament—a series of games played to decide a championship

TO LEARN MORE

AT THE LIBRARY

Killion, Ann. *Champions of Women's Soccer*. New York, N.Y.: Philomel Books, 2018.

Peterson, Megan Cooley. *Soccer's Biggest Moments*. Mankato, Minn.: Black Rabbit Books, 2018.

Savage, Jeff. *US Women's National Team: Soccer Champions*. Minneapolis, Minn.: Lerner Publications, 2019.

ON THE WEB

Learning more about the World Cup is as easy as 1, 2, 3.

1. Go to www.factsurfer.com.

2. Enter "World Cup" into the search box.

3. Click the "Surf" button and you will see a list of related web sites.

With factsurfer.com, finding more information is just a click away.

INDEX

1930 World Cup, 11

1982 World Cup, 12

1991 Women's World Cup, 12

2015 Women's World Cup, 4

Argentina, 11

bracket, 17, 18-19

Brazil, 13

countries, 6, 9, 15, 20

fans, 20, 21

FIFA World Cup Trophy, 6, 7

goal, 5

group stage, 16

Hamm, Mia, 13

hat trick, 5

International Federation of Football Association (FIFA), 6, 7, 10, 12

Japan, 4

knockout stage, 16

Lloyd, Carli, 4, 5

match, 4, 10, 11, 12, 14, 17, 21

Norway, 12

Olympic sport, 10

Pelé, 13

Rapinoe, Megan, 5

regions, 14

round, 14, 16, 17

team, 4, 6, 10, 11, 12, 14, 15, 16, 17, 20, 21

tournament, 6, 9, 10, 11, 12, 14, 15

United States, 4, 5, 8, 11, 12, 13

Uruguay, 11